P9-CLN-048

A ROOKIE READER®

KATIE CAN

By Becky Bring McDaniel

Illustrations by Lois Axeman

Prepared under the direction of Robert Hillerich, Ph.D.

CHILDREN'S PRESS
A Division of Grolier Publishing
Sherman Turnpike
Danbury, Connecticut 06816

For Joyce

Library of Congress Cataloging in Publication Data

McDaniel, Becky Bring.
Katie can.

(A Rookie Reader)
Summary: Although she is too small to roller-skate backwards or ride a bike with no hands, Katie surprises her older brother and sister when she teaches their dog a new trick.
[1. Size—Fiction. 2. Ability—Fiction. 3. Brothers and sisters—Fiction] I. Axeman, Lois, ill. II. Title.
III. Series.
PZ7.M1399Kat 1987 [E] 87-5190
ISBN 0-516-02082-X

Childrens Press, Chicago

Printed in the United States of America.

13 14 15 16 R 02 01

Jenny was the oldest and the biggest.

Kris was the second oldest and the second biggest.

Katie was the youngest and the smallest.

Jenny could ride her bike with no hands.

Kris could ride his bike with no hands.

Katie said, “I can ride my bike with no hands.”

But when everyone came to
see her, she fell off!

Kris could roller-skate backward.

Jenny could roller-skate backward.

Jenny could roller-skate backward.

Kris could roller-skate backward.

Katie said, "I can roller-skate backward."

But when everyone came to see her, she fell down!

Jenny could swim from one side of
the pool to the other without stopping.

Kris could swim from one side of the pool to the other without stopping.

Katie said, “I can swim from one side of the pool to the other without stopping.”

But when everyone came to see her, she stopped three times!

Kris taught the dog to chase a ball.

Jenny taught the dog
to bring the ball back.

Katie said, "I can teach the dog a trick too."

But this time nobody came to see her.

Katie threw the ball up
and the dog caught it.

Katie said, "I taught the dog a new trick and nobody came to see me. Nobody ever comes to see me when I really can do something."

Katie threw the ball again. The dog caught it again. Katie heard some clapping.

When she turned around,
there stood Jenny and Kris.

They did come to see her after all!

WORD LIST

a
after
again
all
and
around
back
backward
ball
biggest
bike
bring
but
came
can
caught
chase
clapping
come
comes
could
did
do
dog
down
ever
everyone
fell
from
hands
heard
her
his
I
it
Jenny
Katie
Kris
me
my
new
no
nobody
of
off
oldest
one
other
pool
really
ride
roller-skate
said
second
see
she
side
smallest
some
something
stood
stopped
stopping
swim
taught
teach
the
there
they
this
three
threw
time
times
to
too
trick
turned
up
was
when
with
without
youngest

About the Author

Becky Bring McDaniel was born September 16, 1953 in Ashland, Ohio. She has lived in Gainesville, Florida since 1970 and traveled to Europe and the Middle East. Her books, *Katie Did It* and *Katie Couldn't*, have been published by Childrens Press in Chicago, Illinois and included in its Rookie Reader Program. Having established herself as a successful writer of children's books and stories, she still pursues her talents as a poet.

Her poetry has been well received thus far and a sampling of the magazines publishing her works include *Writers' Opportunities*, *Creative Years*, the *National Girl Scout Magazine*, *Alura*, and *Whiskey River*. As if these credentials were not enough in their own right, she also has authored an activity puzzle which was published by *High Adventure* magazine.

Currently residing in Gainesville, Florida in order to attend school, she is establishing herself as an artist deemed to be much in demand during the coming years.

About the Artist

Lois Axeman was born and raised in Chicago, Illinois. She studied art in Chicago at the American Academy, Illinois Institute of Technology, and at the Art Institute. She taught illustration at the University of Illinois Circle Campus for four years. The mother of two grown children and grandmother of one, Lois and her husband, Harvey Retzloff, live in a lakefront building where they both pursue their careers in the graphic arts. They share their home with their Shih Tzu dog Marty and their female cat Charlie. Lois uses her children, her grandchild, and her pets as models for her picture book characters. In their spare time Lois and Harvey enjoy painting, playing tennis, and growing orchids.